110 YEARS

WITH

JOSEPHINE

THE HISTORY OF

1856 — 1966

JOSEPHINE COUNTY, OREGON

COPYRIGHT 1966 BY
JOSEPHINE COUNTY HISTORICAL SOCIETY
PRINTED BY KLOCKER PRINTERY, MEDFORD, OREGON

BY JACK SUTTON

TABLE OF CONTENTS

DEDICATION

The Josephine County Historical Society and the author are deeply indebted to the many kind people whose pictures and objects of historical interest made this publication possible. It must be noted, however, that even with the cooperation of this vast number of contributors, it would have been impossible to produce this volume without the dedicated efforts of six men. They are Amos Voorhies and the late Fred Isham (left above), Johnny Vallen (right above), and the Josephine County Court, comprised of Bruce Davidson (left below), Lewis Ringuette (center below), and Don McGregor (right below).

Jack Sutton

I.
SETTLEMENT

The first white men to pass through the Rogue Valley were groups of Hudson's Bay trappers. The Hudson's Bay Company's red and white flag (above) flew from an outpost near Yreka which claimed as its trapping domain the areas of northern California and southern Oregon. The company's official coat-of-arms carried the Latin motto "pro pelle cutum" (left below). Translated literally, this phrase means " a skin for a skin". The actual interpretation intended would read: "he (the fur trapper) risks his skin (cutum) for a skin (pelle)". According to the company's records, fifteen brigades of trappers passed through the Rogue Valley (right below) between the years of 1825 and 1843.

One of the reports (left above) of Hudson's Bay trappers, under Alexander Roderick McLeod, is credited with naming of the Siskiyou Mountains to commemorate loss of bobtailed horses in that region. In 1836, Ewing Young drove a herd of cattle over the Siskiyous and through the valley enroute to the Willamette (right above). In 1841, an expedition under Lt. Emmons followed the Hudson's Bay trail from Fort Vancouver to the Sacramento Valley crossing the Rogue River at present Fort Vannoy (below).

In 1846, a wagon train left the Old Oregon Trail at Fort Hall to try a new route laid out by Jesse and Lindsay Applegate (above). Just north of the Grave Creek bridge (left below), the wagon train rested before attempting the remaining barriers of the Umpqua and Calapooya Mountains. A fourteen year old girl, named Martha Leland Crowley, died and was buried beneath an oak tree which stood in the present roadway (right below) and the creek received the name which it bears today from this event. A map showing the route of the Applegate trail is shown at the top of page 5. Due to the hardships encountered by the original party following this route, the trail was bitterly denounced by Governor George Abernathy in an 1847 circular letter.

CIRCULAR.

TO THE OREGON EMIGRANTS.

GENTLEMEN:

It being made my duty, as Superintendent of Indian affairs, by an Act passed by the Legislature of Oregon, "to give such instructions and directions to Emigrants to this Territory, in regard to their conduct towards the natives, by the observance of which, they will be most likely to maintain and promote peace and friendship between them and the Indian tribes through which they may pass," allow me to say in the first place, that the Indians on the old road to this country, are friendly to the whites. They should be treated with kindness on all occasions. As Indians are inclined to steal, keep them out of your camps. If one or two are admitted, watch them closely. Notwithstanding the Indians are friendly, it is best to keep in good sized companies while passing through their country. Small parties of two or three are sometimes stripped of their property while on their way to this Territory, perhaps because a preceding party promised to pay the Indians for something had of them, and failed to fulfil their promise. This will show you the necessity of keeping your word with them in all cases.

There is another subject upon which I would say a few words. A number of the emigrants of 1845 took a cut off, as it is called, to shorten the route, leaving the old road; the consequence was, they were later getting in, lost their property, and many lost their lives. Some of those who reached the settlements, were so broken down by sickness, that it was so many months before they recovered sufficient strength to labor.

A portion of the emigrants of 1846 took a new route, called the southern route. This proved very disastrous to all those who took it. Some of the emigrants that kept on the old road, reached this place as early as the 13th of September, with their wagons, and all got in, in good season, with their wagons and property, I believe, except a few of the last party. While those that took the southern route, were very late in reaching the settlements—they all lost more or less of their property—many of them losing all they had and barely getting in with their lives; a few families were obliged to winter in the Umpqua mountains, not being able to reach the settlements.

I would therefore recommend you to keep the old road. A better way may be found, but it is not best for men with wagons and families to try the experiment.

My remarks are brief, but I hope may prove beneficial to you.

Dated at Oregon City, this 22d of April, 1847.

GEO. ABERNETHY,
GOVERNOR OF OREGON TERRITORY AND
SUPERINTENDENT OF INDIAN AFFAIRS.

A portion of the original Applegate Trail was mentioned in the Immigrants' Guide to Oregon and California written in 1845 by Landford Hastings (left above). In 1851, Josephine Rollins Ort (right above), after whom the county is named, came to the Illinois Valley with her father, Floyd Rollins and other prospectors. This has been credited as the first discovery of gold in southern Oregon. The party was led to a site on Josephine Creek (below) by Indians they had met near Vannoy Crossing.

Between the years of 1850 and 1857, Josephine County was plagued by Indian Wars. Some of the grave stone markers indicated the death of early settlers at the hands of the Indians. McDonough Harkness (left above) is buried in the Croxton Cemetery near Lincoln School. He was killed while carrying dispatches from the Galice area to the fort at Grave Creek. William Guest (right above) was shot with his own rifle while plowing his field in the Deer Creek region and is buried in the cemetery at Deer Creek. The Indian wars were fought by volunteers and regular troops stationed at Fort Jones, California; Fort Lane, near Medford; and Fort Orford in Curry County. The regular army wore uniforms such as are depicted below. The "dragoons" of these wars were heavily armed, mounted infantrymen (right below).

At Harris Flat just north of Manzanita Park Rest on Highway 5, stood a cabin owned by George Harris whose wife, Mary Anne, fought off the Indians in one of Oregon's most dramatic actions on "the bloody day of October 9, 1855". In the Jacksonville museum, one of the guns used by Mrs. Harris in the defense of her home is displayed (right above). In this battle, Mrs. Harris's daughter (right above) was wounded. A book written by Riddle (for whom Riddle, Oregon is named) depicted the Indian attack as shown below.

Fort Vannoy at Vannoy Crossing (left above) served as one of the prime recruiting posts for volunteers. On the Illinois River near Agnes can be found the site of the final peace treaty meeting which was held just before the last battles of the 1855 war (right above). The Indians were moved to the Grand Rhonde and Siletz reservations. A picture of some of Siletz Indians (below) was taken by the late Amos Voorhies, editor of the Grants Pass Courier.

Fort Briggs

A bill to separate what is now Josephine County from Jackson County was introduced to the territorial legislature by George Briggs (above) who had just been elected a representative by the voters of Jackson County. The bill was passed and approved on January 22, 1856. Waldo, first known as Sailor Diggin's, which boasted of several stores, a number of saloons, billiard halls and hotels, was named the county seat of Josephine County (below and page 11).

Waldo Oregon in 1861

The rubble shown above was all that remained of the town of Waldo a few years ago. Even this has now disappeared into the brush and undergrowth.

The old general merchandise store which stood on this location had been built in 1863 and is shown below as it appeared in 1902.

The back of the Decker store appears in the foreground of the old Waldo picture above (left). At the front of the store (right above) was the customary hitching rack and flag pole common to this period. The ground on which the town of Waldo had stood was not mined in the early days and when it became a deserted area, as shown below, the hydraulic giants were moved in to work the ground for its gold.

Main St. Waldo, Ore. Early Mining Camp.

The last business man to operate the Waldo store was George Elder (left above). Though it was planned to save this remaining relic of the town, a blast of the giants reduced the final store to a pile of locally made brick (right above). In 1919, a land development company endeavored to sell speculation lots in the town and began construction of a hotel (below) which was never completed.

Kirbyville, old County Seat on Josephine County, Oregon.

In 1857, the county seat was moved to Kerby (above). One of the oldest county warrants known to exist is shown below. Though it was issued in July, 1859 exactly six months after Oregon had become a state, the document still bore the heading of "Oregon Territory".

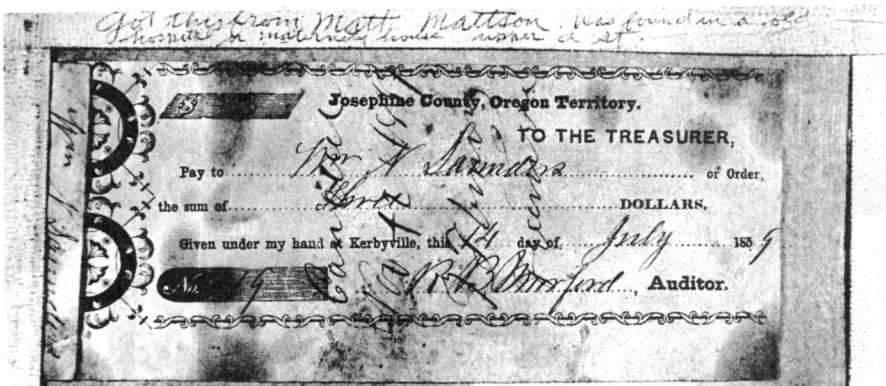

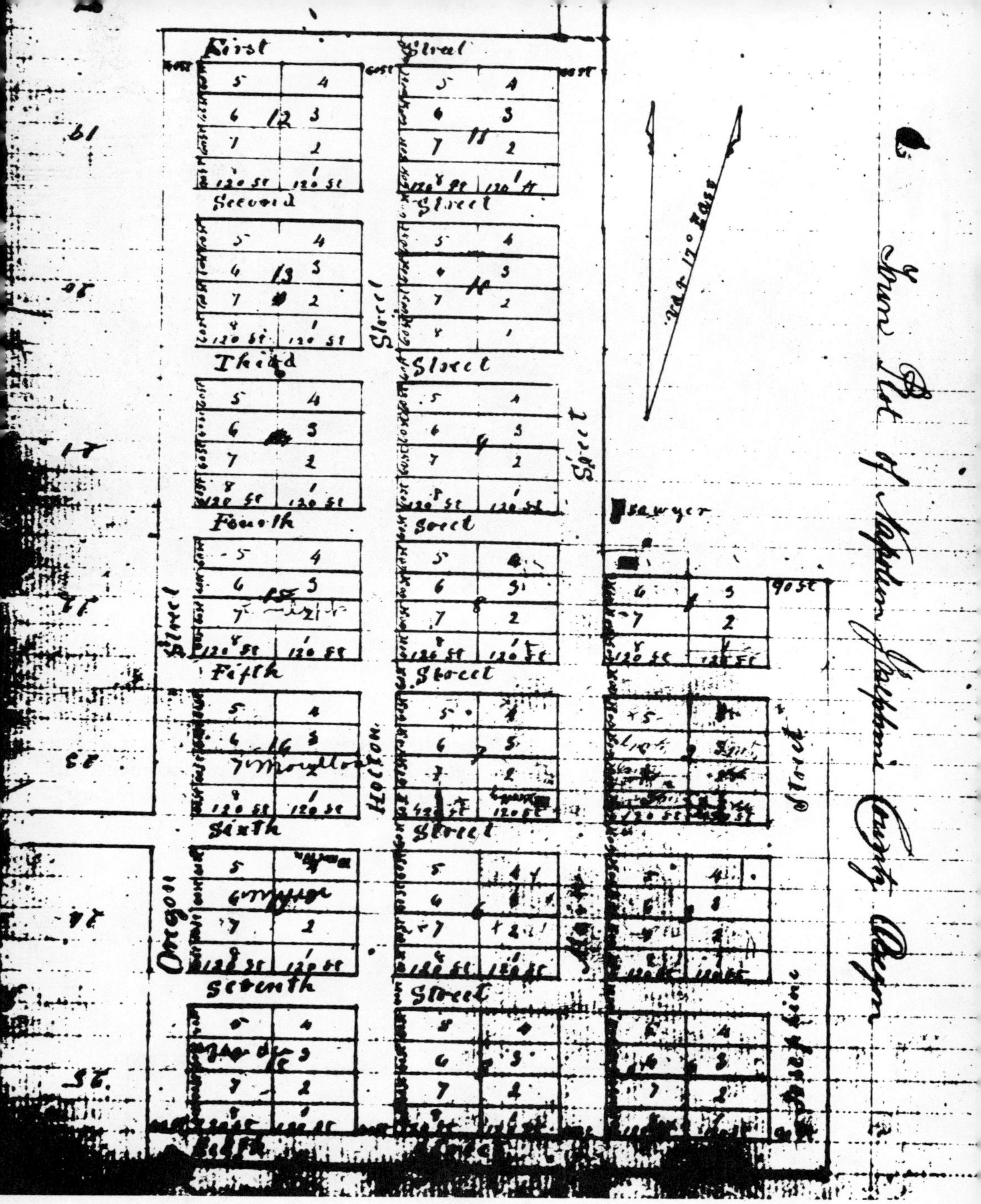

The original plat of Kerby, then called "Napoleon" and so approved by the state legislature of 1859, is shown above. The name of Kerbyville was chosen in honor of the original Donation Land Grant claimant, Dr. Holton who selected the new name, contended that "Josephine (County) should have her 'Napoleon'".

The county's first jail was built at Kerby (above). The log structure, later covered with clapboards, contained six cells. The two views of Kerby presented below, depict the changes of a sixty year span in the life of Josephine County's second seat of government.

GRANTS PASS ORE...

SOUTH STREET LOOKING
SOUTH FROM RAILROAD

Motivated primarily by the desire to gain a railhead, the state legislature was petitioned in 1885 to change the boundary between Josephine and Jackson Counties to place Grants Pass within the boundaries of Josephine (see inside of front cover). In the June election of 1886, three towns were considered by the voters for the new county seat. These were: Kerby, Wilderville, and Grants Pass. The latter received a majority of 116 votes in the 716 ballots cast. In the view below, we see Grants Pass as it would have appeared from Foundry and G Streets looking east in the mid 1880's.

The first courthouse in Grants Pass (above) was built and commissioned in 1886 at a cost of $2,400.00. The county jail at the rear of the wooden structure was contracted for $334.00. The 1917 building, still in use, (below) stands on the same ground as the original building.

III.
GRANTS PASS

Long before Grants Pass became a stage station, the log house at Perkins' Ferry near White Rock Riffle (above) served as the Perkinsville voting precinct for Jackson County. The scene shown below was taken at the corner of Sixth and G Streets looking west.

The railroad station at the left of the picture above stood in the middle of Sixth Street and was later moved by railroad flat car to Merlin. This view shows G Street before the trees and stumps had been removed. The picture below was taken at the corner of Fifth and G Streets looking east.

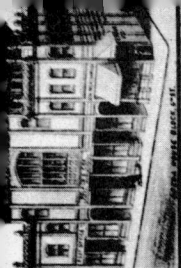

BIRDSEYE VIEW OF **GRANTS PASS**, OREGON.

COUNTY SEAT OF JOSEPHINE COUNTY, FOUNDED 1884, POPULATION 1889 3000

PUBLISHED AUGUST 1890

LINCOLN PARK

VILLA ADDITION

GRANTS PASS NURSERY, W. E. BLACKBURN, PROP.

FINEST RESIDENT PROPERTY IN GRANTS PASS. ARTHUR CONKLIN

RESIDENCE OF J. E. MOON.

LAYTONS HYDRAULIC MINING NEAR GRANTS PASS R.

THE BRUNSWICK HOTEL, COR. MAIN & G STREETS. I. A. MILLER, PROP.

WESTERN HOTEL

SHERER & JUDSON.

PARKER & JUDSONS NEW BLOCK, G ST.

WESTERN HOTEL, H & 6 STS.

LIBRARY & FEED STABLE, G ST.

SASH, DOOR & BLIND FACTORY

Long before the air age became a reality, artist's conceptions of birdseye views were drawn. The scene on page 22 was prepared in 1890. At the turn of the century, a huge box kite (upper right) was flown from Tokay Heights with a camera attached (center right) to obtain an actual aerial photograph (below) of Grants Pass. A panoramic view of the Rogue Valley duplicated from a Commercial Club folder of 1910 is presented on pages 24 and 25.

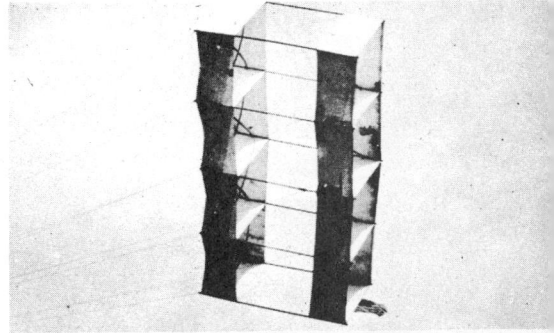

Birdseye view of Grants Pass Ore 10702.

PANORAMIC VIEW OF THE ROGUE RIVER VALLEY, SHOWING ESPECIALLY JOSEPHINE CO

The lens of the finest camera or the pen of the most skilled draughtsman are alike in
its broad and fertile fields, its rounded hills and its setting of rugged, forest-clad mountains.
this noble valley. Nothing that goes to make life worth living has been omitted. Nowhere
all those utilitarian elements, lacking which, even the Garden of Eden must have remained
the roots which are necessary for the life of man and the animals he has domesticated to hi
of mankind. Over all is bent the azure bow of a perfect sky, which yields moisture
where the joy of living and the need of making a living are not

...TY AND THE LOCATION OF GRANTS PASS RELATIVE TO THE TRIBUTARY COUNTRY

...able of producing a true picture of this garden-like valley, with its beautiful water-ways, ...urely the One who made the earth as well as the heaven used His highest skill in forming ...the face of Nature presented in lovelier aspect. And with all the loveliness, there are too, ...inhabited. Here the soil produces bountifully of the grains and the grasses, the fruit and ...se. And in the earth are stored the metals and minerals precious or useful for the arts ...d sunshine as they are needed. Here is a land of richness, a land of pure delight, ...compatible, a haven the like of which is hardly to be found.

From the 1860 stage station located on Seventh Street north of Savage, Grants Pass moved to the area beside the railroad right of way developing first on Foundry Street shown at the right of the top picture. Due to the nationality of the original owner, this section became known as "Little Jerusalem" while the area pictured in the scene below on G Street was called "Jericho". The latter site selection was proven to be the most desirable for business development and before many years had passed became the prime business district of the town (below).

The two stores shown on this page (Smith's Variety Store below) were among the early business houses on G Street.

The first Odd Fellows Hall was located on Foundry but moved to this more spacious building (above) on the southeast corner of H and Sixth Streets shortly after Grants Pass became the Josephine County seat. In the picture below, the winter problems of mud on Sixth Street were still much in evidence at the turn of the century.

A familiar sight of the times were the horse drawn delivery carts such as that employed by Calhoun's Grocery in the picture above. The issuance of intoxicating liquor licenses was restricted in 1905 to allow one saloon to each 500 persons of its population. Prior to this time, an adequate supply of such refreshment centers existed along G Street between Fourth and Sixth (below).

On the east side of Sixth Street, in the railroad right-of-way between G and the tracks, a city park was laid out complete with flag pole and bandstand (above). Beside the building, then serving as the city hall (now the Golden Rule), stood the Lister and Calvert Livery Stable to which customers could walk on a spacious wooden boardwalk (below).

Shortly after the turn of the century, store patrons could do their shopping on cement sidewalks without getting their shoes muddy or dusty until it was necessary to cross Sixth Street.

In the picture shown above, the camera was placed in the center of Sixth Street midway between I and J Streets. The merchants on the south side of the tracks were soon provided competition by the development of that area north of F Street (below).

The first building to occupy the northwest corner of F Street was Bagley's Hotel which was later renamed the Western Hotel and moved two blocks north on the east side of Sixth (at left of picture below).

NO.2 6ST LOOKING SOUTH GRANTS PASS ORE ON "THE ROAD OF A THOUSAND WONDERS"

The Josephine Hotel (now the Redwoods) for a brief time was the only
commercial building standing between
E Street and the courthouse (above).
A later scene is shown below.

The view above shows Sixth Street looking west from the roof of the old Josephine Hotel. The 1902 Masonic building at the left of the picture below stood on the southeast corner of E and Sixth Streets.

In the short span of ten years, the block between E and F changed from the sight familiar to oldtime residents (above) to that shown below.

The arrival of the automobile age presented few parking problems to Grants Pass, though the winter mud still tended to discourage many motorists.

With the increase of automobile traffic, a more efficient means of increasing available parking facilities had to be devised and automobiles were backed into parking spaces as shown above.

Since long bedded trucks created a major problem for pedestrians on the sidewalks, the procedure was reversed at a later date as we see below.

"It's The Climate"
GRANTS PASS, OREGON

Today's view of Sixth Street north from the roof of the Wing Building (above). View looking south (below).

G Street (once called Front Street) looking west (above).

The U. S. National Bank originally occupied the southwest corner of 6th and G Streets (left).

As the latter corner appears today (below).

G Street from the roof of the Wing Building (right). View of G Street east (left below). Northeast corner of Sixth and G Streets (right below).

IV.
SCHOOLS AND CHURCHES

The Gimmett School (above) which served as the Sucker Creek School District #41 before the turn of the century is believed to be the only log school house in Oregon reassembled for historic preservation. It is now displayed for the benefit of visitors at Josephine County's museum in Kerby.

Officially titled School District #43 of Jackson County, this first Grants Pass School stood near Ninth and Savage Streets (below).

OFF FOR A MONTH.

Nearly all early schools served a dual role as public and religious education institutions. Services were conducted by "circuit rider" ministers such as T. L. Jones (left above) who gave his ser-mons in the first school of present Grants Pass (right above). The faded picture shown below is believed to be the earliest taken of a Grants Pass student body.

Grants Pass School, taugh by W W Fidler 1870'

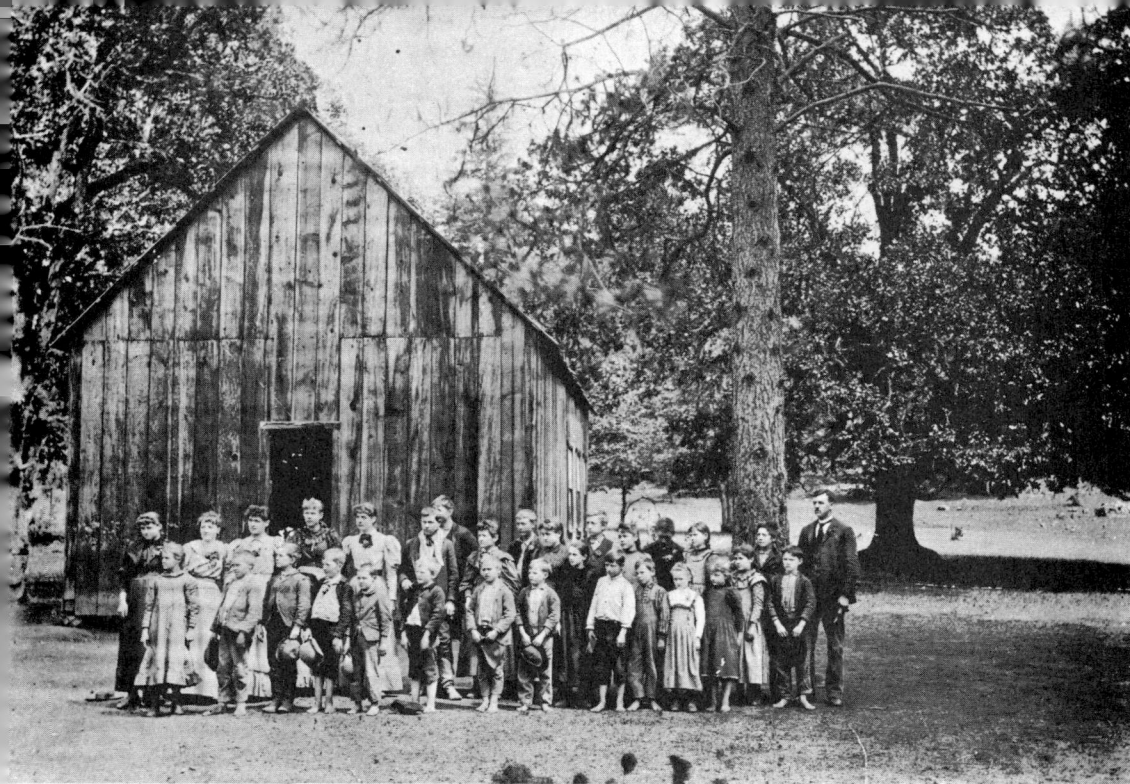

Typical of the schools throughout the Rogue Valley is this one shown above with the schoolmaster holding the bell and his charges posing proudly for their class picture. It is interesting to note that the majority of the boys are bare-footed. The Centennial School pictured below was built at Fruitdale during the year of the 100th anniversary of the signing of the Declaration of Independence.

Grants Pass, still a part of Jackson County, began its first educational expansion in 1884 with the purchase of a two story community meeting building from Jerome Prairie. The building was moved to the site of the present Washington School and renamed Central School. In 1885, the school opened with a student body of 100 pupils, but by 1888 had expanded to the point that a west wing had to be added (below).

Picture made in 1888

EUREKA HIGH SCHOOL

—OF—

Thorough and Practical Instruction, near Wilderville, Josephine County, Oregon, Will commence its first session,

October 4, 1886, To Continue Six Months.

———RATES OF TUITION:———

Primary Branches, $4.00 per Quarter.

Intermediate Branches $6.00 per Quarter.

High Arithmatic, Natural Philosophy, Mediaeval and Modern History, Physical Geography, Botany and Retoric, $7.00 per Quarter.

Algebra, Chemistry, Astronomy, Geology, Moral Philosophy, Mental Philosophy, Physiology and Hygine, and Ancient History $7.50 per Quarter.

Geometry, and the Higher Mathematics, Book-keeping, Latin, and the Principles of the German Language $9.00.

Board including Room, Lights, &c., $2.50 per week.

Unfurnished Rooms free to Students boarding themselves.

The School Room will be furnished with Good Seets, Wall Maps, Globes and Cubical Blocks ; also

PHILOSOPHICAL AND CHEMICAL APPARATUS.

as the necesities of the Scoool demand them.

None will be allowed to attend Dances while Students of the School.

STRICT DISCIPLINE WILL BE MAINTAINED.

Special Inducements Afforded to those Preparing to Teach.

No pains or expense will be spared to make the School equal to any in Southern Oregon, in point of

Thoroughness and Practical Work.

Good produce taken in part pay.   Patronage Solicited.

JOHN H. ROBINSON, Principal.

The advertisement above was published for the first high school in Josephine County.

About 1900, the fireman's recreation room of the city hall was pressed into service as a classroom for sixty-five fifth grade boys. The room was the upstairs section of the present Golden Rule Store. The arrangement did not prove satisfactory since it became great sport to throw rocks at the prisoners in the jail cells below. For this purpose, the young men brought their own rocks to class. Additional problems were created for the volunteer fire group who frowned upon the playful ringing of the alarm bell by these same energetic fifth graders.

Architecture for the one room school-houses throughout the county remained very much the same until the 1920's, though a few "modernizing" touches such as porches were added as shown below.

ST. LUKES EPISCOPAL CHURCH

UNITED PRESBYTERIAN CHURCH

EAST SIDE SCHOOL

CENTRAL SCHOOL

RIVERSIDE SCHOOL

The Commercial Club publication of 1910 shows pictures of churches and schools in Grants Pass at that particular period. It is interesting to note, however, that there were only four schools rather than the five depicted and the one titled "East Side School" and "Public School, Grants Pass, Oregon" in the center are one and the same building.

The Grants Pass High School (above) and the Illinois Valley High School (below) present a picture of far more efficient educational institutions than the Eureka High School (left) of early years.

The first church built in Grants Pass was the Methodist Episcopal (left above). After the bell tower had been blown down by the wind storm of 1890, the present structure was erected on the same ground. The Bridgeview Church (right above) served in a unique capacity during the days of prohibition when it was said the facility was used to house a still. In those days before the establishment of funeral parlors, churches were always employed in the final services for the deceased (below).

The Grants Pass City Band (above) was organized in 1886 and made its first official debut in 1887, though prior to that time it performed in a few parades such as the one shown below.

Shown above is the 1927 Grants Pass
Band, complete with their resplendent
uniforms. The early bands performed
in the Grants Pass Opera House, completed in 1891 (below).

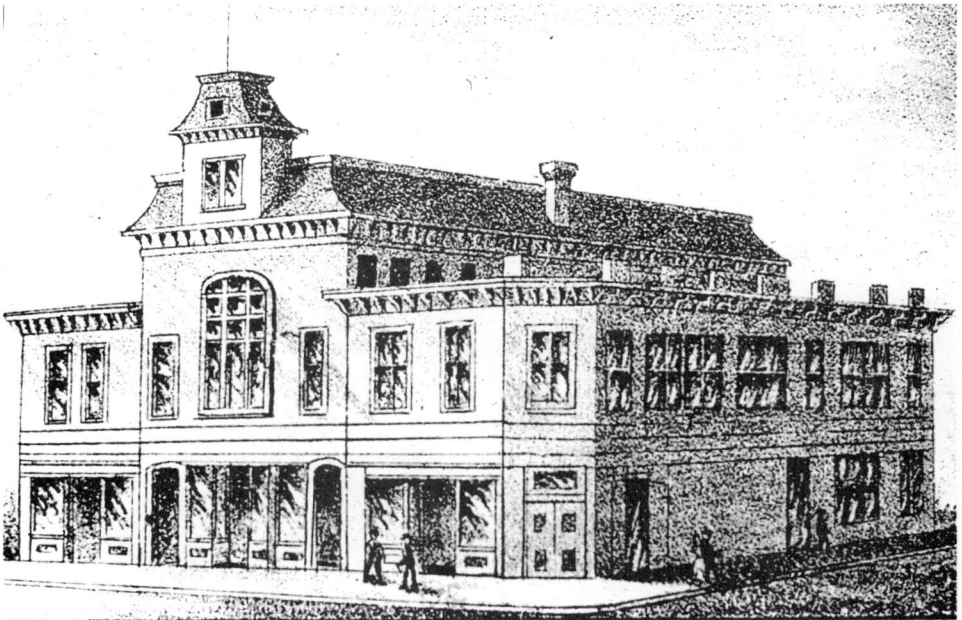

The view above shows the Opera House at the right of the picture. The hands of the clock on the tower of the bank across the street are stopped, as was the custom of this period, at the hour of President Lincoln's death. The inside of the Opera House with its flag draped boxes is shown below.

SYNOPSIS.

ACT I.—Court of the Queen of the Universe; opening chorus, "All Hail," chorus of Fairies; they beg the Queen of the Universe to choose them a Sovereign, Virtue's plan; "A Mortal dear to me has been led astray by evil spirits." "Let Honor, Wealth and Love bestow their best gifts on this fallen man, and she who reclaims him shall be the Fairy Queen!" Chorus, "Lo, Night appears," Vesper Hymn. Tableau.

ACT II.—Evil Spirits and Demons. Drinking Chorus. Vice and his followers boast of what they can do. The Duke of Burgundy is lured to his ruin. Song and Chorus. Tableau.

ACT III.—Leperello, the Valet, who is always hungry. Remorse of the Duke. "My fortune gone, deserted by my friends, forsaken by Heaven itself, I am indeed most wretched." Fairy Rosalie, with song and dance. Chorus of Fairies, Solo, "Triumphant Honor Comes." Fairies bestow the gifts of Honor upon the Duke. Farewell chorus. Tableau.

ACT IV.—Despair of the Duke. Saved. Chorus of Fairies, with Rose Dance. Solo, "Mortal, Heat Me." Shower of Gold. Leperello gets a square meal at last. Fairy dance, Youth Beauty and Pleasure. "Fare Thee Well." Chorus and Tableau.

ACT V.—Leperello tells how his master lost his Wealth. The Demons exult over the ruin they have wrought. Demons' Dance. Goddess of Love and Cupid. Solo, "Love's Sorrow." Cupid plants true love in the mortal's heart. Solo, "Power of Love." Love's triumph. Cupid's Tricks. Spanish Dance. Leperello and his Evelina.

ACT VI.—Vulcan and Hercules. Vice is sentenced to everlasting banishment. Crowning Scene, Love, the Queen of the fairies. TABLEAU FINALE.

Grants Pass Opera House
WEDNESDAY EVENING, JULY 29, 1896.

GRAND PRODUCTION OF BEAUTIFUL OPERETTA

TRIUMPH OF LOVE
SIXTY PERFORMERS—ALL HOME TALENT

Elegant Costumes   Delightful Music   Charming Tableaux
Beautiful Fairy Dances

MRS. L. NEUMAYER — DIRECTRESS
MRS. BELL HUDEN — PIANIST
H. ANDERSON, San Francisco — COSTUMER
GRANTS PASS CORNET BAND

PRESS NOTES

The Libretto of the "Triumph of Love" is the work of Mrs. L. Neumayer. The music she has called here and there—gems from operas, old German airs, etc., and put together in a most charming arrangement of plot and harmony, bright and sparkling throughout. During the past ten years Mrs Neumayer has produced her Operetta in every city and town on the Pacific Coast, and recently in Colorado. A few newspaper extracts are given below:

The Grand Opera House was crowded last night to witness the second performance of the "Triumph of Love," under Mrs. L. Neumayer's management. A thoroughly delightful performance.

* * * * The merry music, gay costumes, charming tableaux, and humorous situations, all conspire to render the "Triumph of Love" as pleasing as anything of the kind we have ever seen.—Los Angeles Express.

The benefit for the Congregational church drew a crowded house last night. The "Triumph of Love" is beautiful in conception, sentiment and language, and as pleasing as anything of the kind we have ever seen.—Santa Cruz Sentinel

The Appeal and Marysville people generally heartily recommended Mrs. Neumayer and her pretty operetta to our neighbors on the north.—Marysville Appeal

CALHOUN BROS., Grants Pass, Or.

Many of the productions presented in the Opera House were performances of home talent as may be noted in the program above. With the purchase of the building by the First National Bank of Oregon, the long condemned Opera House was demolished in 1955 (below).

The Grants Pass Water, Light, and Power Company began construction of this power dam (above) a short distance down stream from Caveman Bridge in 1889. The dam was also used to provide water to hydrants for city needs, and through the summer months some of the dust was settled on Sixth Street by the sprinkler shown below.

As fire fighting apparatus improved over the years, the Grants Pass Fire Department moved into more spacious quarters and occupied what is today the Grants Pass City Hall (below). The Kerby fire fighting gear was rather unique (right).

FIRE STATION GRANTS PASS ORE.

The Grants Pass Commercial Club (above) was organized in 1907 to serve the same purpose as the later Chamber of Commerce, established in 1924 (left).

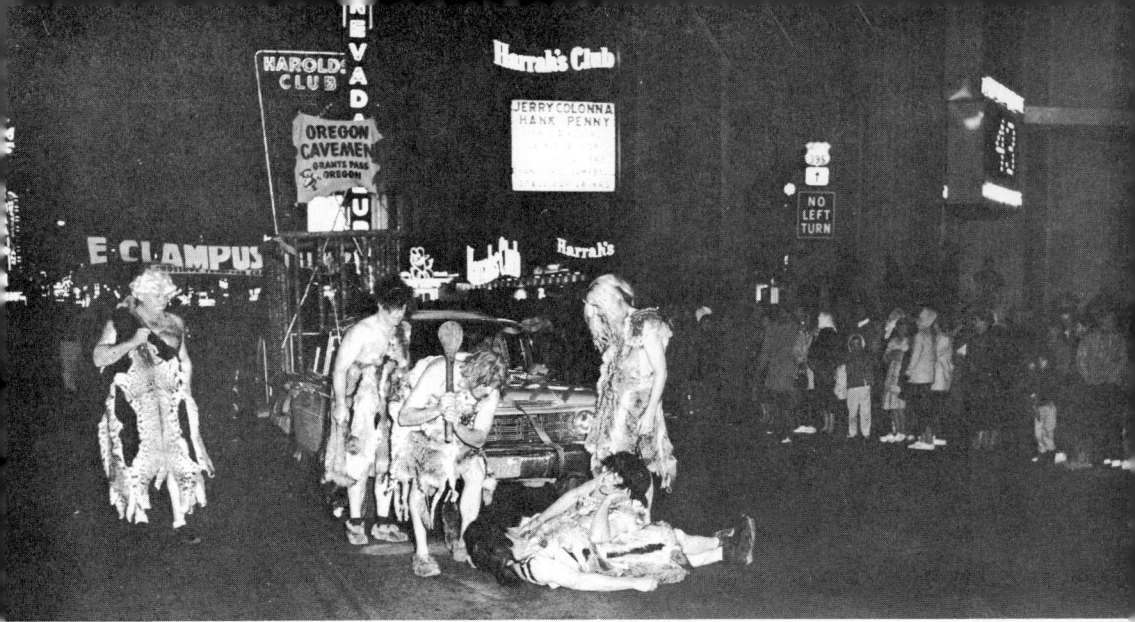

One of the most widely acclaimed and world famous booster clubs is Josephine County's own Oregon Cavemen, conceived and organized in 1922. The antics of this energetic group have ranged from simple blocking of traffic, as shown above, to the design of unique transits (left below) assembled in 1927 to bid on the building of the San Francisco-Oakland Bay Bridge (which they offered to construct for a fee of 23,756,000 deer hides). Even Sally Rand's show at the San Francisco World's Fair was invaded by the Chief Big Horn and his tribe (right below) in 1939.

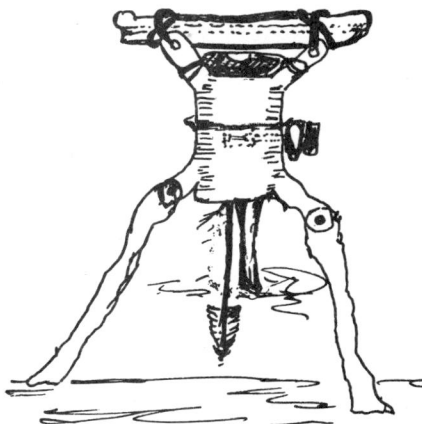

The Cavemen became internationally famous with their initiation of Governor Dewey during his 1948 presidential campaign as shown above. Russian news-papers used this picture to show their people how the rich "cavort" in America (below).

SA-POLITIKER als Höhlenmensche

er wie prominente Amerikaner, die Beschimpfer europäischer Kultur, ihre Freizeit verbring

Licedoc polítici americani cho teneo riso de jngolesth Cisné pedencat americani, designatori della sludé europea, traescorrono la loro dire al reposo

Políticos de los RRUU, como hombres de los cavernas. Y por como los americanos prominentes, los dimonadores de la cultura europea, emplean sus ratos de ocio

Stalin Apes Hitler—That Joseph Stalin imitates Adolp Hitler in his effort to ridicule the United States is shown b these two pictures. When Thomas Dewey visited Oregon i the presidential primary campaign in 1948 he was enter tained by the Grants Pass Cavemen, and the picture, at tor appeared in the Oregonian. It is now being used in Russi

Nearly every presidential hopeful (above) and governors of Oregon, including Mark Hatfield (below), have had the "pleasure" of drinking the Cavemen's "dinosaur's blood".

The first Josephine County public library, initially established in the old Sixth Street City Hall, made its first permanent quarters in the Carnegie sponsored building shown at the left in the above picture. The beautiful new home is shown at the right above and in the scene below.

The tremendous growth of county business during the past decade necessitated the addition of wings to the old 1917 courthouse as shown above. The population explosion experienced by the county is also in evidence when we look at the early hospital shown to the right and the outdated facilities of Josephine General Hospital (below) which have been superseded by the building at the left edge of the same picture.

The new Josephine County Hospital, shown above, represents Josephine's most recent endeavor in the field of public service and community development. Modern dental clinics contrast sharply with early offices in both interior furnishings and equipment. The patient of yesteryear had to endure the potential variations in the dentist's drilling speed which could vary with his foot weariness. As early as 1905, Josephine County was unique in offering the services of a woman dentist (Mrs. Floyd of Kerby) shown at the right below.

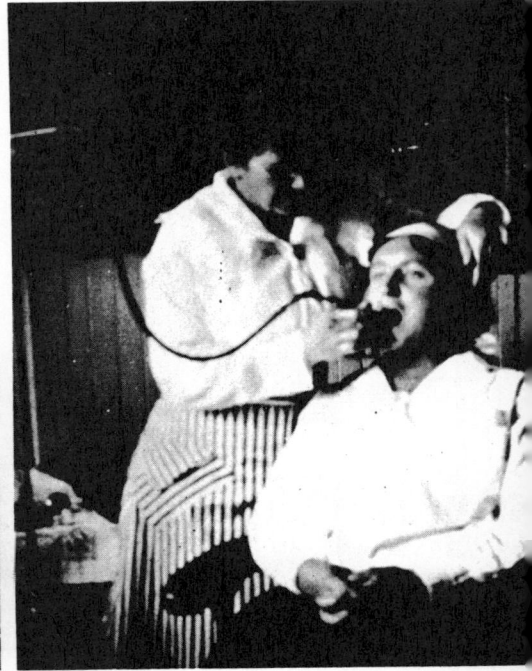

A coverage of the medical profession would not be complete without inclusion of the early barber shops which served for all minor surgery, such as the removal of boils, warts, ingrown hair, etc. The Kerby shop shown above was typical of the average at the turn of the century. In the 1920's Josephine County began to turn its attention to improvement of tourist facilities which could also be enjoyed by the local citizenry (below).

In Auto Camp Grounds
Grants Pass Oregon

VI.
COMMUNICATION

That early travelers spoke in terms of "days of travel" between towns within the county of Josephine, seems strange when one views today's highways. Riding the stage of that day made even a trip from Waldo to Grants Pass long and arduous. It was far more simple to send letters for goods needed or for brief communications to friends by U. S. Mail stagecoaches (left above) than to make personal contact. The last of these carriers has been allowed to decay quietly at the psuedo town of Pottsville (right above). The early stage stations like the one at Waldo shown below, served as the pickup points for letters and packages in many of Josephine's small communities.

The Sawyer Hotel (above) was built at Kerbyville in the late 1850's and for many years later saw service as the Pioneer Hotel. The Anderson Stage Station (below), originally named Fort Hay, was the scene of an Indian attack during the 1855 Indian uprising. This stage station stood northeast of present Selma.

Mail destined for Slate Creek was delivered at the old Jones Hotel (above) in Wilderville which for many years served as the meeting center of that community. In these years, Wilderville served as a crossroads point, much as Grants Pass today, with traffic bound for Murphy following the route of the Applegate at this junction. The Wilderville store is shown below.

The Murphy Post Office (above) received its mail by the conveyance shown below until the stage line to Williams was established. The latter service was also the means of mail delivery to Provolt (left).

The station which once served the northern portion of Josephine County is the Wolf Creek Tavern (above). The original portion of this structure was completed in 1857. The Twogood and Harkness House (below) at Grave Creek, still stands as a private residence. This station served also as a stopover point on the main stagecoach line after having seen service in the Indian Wars as a military fort.

The above view shows the mail and passenger stage in front of the Galice Store. The lower picture is an interior view of the general store.

In the picture above, the Galice stage is shown crossing the Rogue River at Massie Ferry near present Indian Mary Park. Indian Mary's cabin may be seen in the background. The first ferry on the Rogue River was operated by a man named Long. That installation was pur-chased by James Vannoy, whose name the crossing still bears and whose grave may be found in the tiny cemetery within the boundaries of the mint farm adjoining the Riverbanks road. Vannoy's grave stone and that of his wife, Margaret, are shown below.

Other ferries operating on the Rogue River were established near the present Robertson Bridge and Griffin Park. The former (above) was known as Lower Ferry, while the Griffin ferry was referred to as the Upper Ferry (below).

Many years after the building of bridges across the Rogue, ferries were still pressed into service as we see from this picture of the 1920's (above). Many walking bridges spanned the rivers and creeks of Josephine and the one shown at left was used in early Kerby. The first Grants Pass bridge was lost in the flood of 1890. In the picture below, we see the second and third bridges to span the Rogue River before the removal of bridge number two.

The third bridge was replaced in 1931 by Caveman Bridge seen above, while still in process of construction. When the county was at last linked by fairly adequate roads and bridges, news was more easily distributed by means of newspapers instead of mail carried dispatches. With the issuance of the Diamond Edition, representing seventy-five years of service as editor of the Grants Pass Courier (left below), Amos Voorhies (right below) retired from public life. Voorhies, acknowledged as one of the deans of Oregon journalism, did more to promote interest in history than any other single individual in the Rogue Valley. He is shown (right below) transcribing his reminiscences on tape.

SUBSCRIBE FOR THE ARGUS!

THE FIRST NEWSPAPER EVER PUBLISHED IN JOSEPHINE COUNTY.

Soon to be ENLARGED——Bold, Fearless and Aggressive.

JOB PRINTING OF ALL KINDS AT THE LOWEST RATES.

The Only Newspaper Published in Josephine County, T... Patronage sufficient to enable it to be printed at home.

SUBSCRIPTION,

The first newspaper to be published in Josephine County was the Argus (above) which was a four page sheet, six by eight inches in size. The unit was printed one page at a time on a small hand press and was first issued March 13, 1885.

The Argus lasted only a few months and appeared at rather irregular intervals during that time. Four of the pages from the October 22nd, 1885 issue are shown on this page.

Three weeks after the Argus had begun publication, another newspaper under the name Grant's Pass Courier (the apostrophe was then used in the city's name) produced its first issue. Through its first six years of existence, the Courier had seven owners and publishers. The above picture shows the press room of the Courier in 1900 when it was located on G Street two doors east of Fifth. In 1909, a lot was purchased on Sixth Street and by the fall of 1934 had been expanded as we see below. "Boss" Voorhies is shown at left with the latest typesetter of that day.

The newspapers of 1897 carried the story of the first legal hanging (right) in Josephine County. While the noose was being adjusted around the neck of L. W. Nelson (left below), he confessed to the murder of Charles Perry, whose body he dropped in an abandoned well west of Kerby. The 32 caliber murder gun is shown at the right below. The victim and murderer are shown in the center of the picture at the lower portion of the page while a piece of the hanging rope adorns the frame.

SIXTH STREET

FIFTH STREET

Jennings and Dean
Heberlee
Lampson
Old Butcher Shop
Ike Wright's Saloon
Pioneer Hotel
Dixon and Son
Fetsch's Saloon
Smith's Shoe Store
Lempke's Beer Hall
Smith and Guild
Glidden's Restaurant
Lempke
Conklin
Cigar Factory

R. R. Depot

Early in the morning of January 11, 1894, eight business houses on G Street (above) burned to the ground in less than 45 minutes. Another fire in 1902 destroyed the first box factory of Grants Pass (below).

BURNING OF THE BOX FACTORY AT GRANTS PASS OREGON

MAY 26TH 1902   M R   PHOTO

AFTER THE FIRE   JULY 14   1902
CITY HOTEL   AND   BREWERY

Less than two months after the box factory had been destroyed, another fire on G Street further changed the Grants Pass scene and the last major fire catastrophe was experienced in 1907 with the loss of many buildings on G between Fourth and Fifth (below).

The Daily Bulletin.

VOL. I.   GRANTS PASS, OREGON TUESDAY, MAY 10, 1898.   NO. 22.

SPANISH ADMIRAL MONTEGO KILLED AFTER ESCAPING FROM CAVITE.

Riot in Progress at Manila and Dewey Unable to Control the Insurgents--Mines Destroyed.

Spain Purchases Two More Warships--Bread Riots in Spain Oregon Food in Cuba.

War Conference

Special to the BULLETIN.

Washington, May 10.—A conference was held today by Secretary Alger and Generals Willis and Corbin. It was decided to put sixty thousand troops in Cuba within ten days.

An attack was ordered on Havana today.

Cable Cut.

Special to the BULLETIN.

Washington, May 10.—The cutting of the South American cable yesterday, has great significance.

Cuban Riots.

Special to the BULLETIN.

Key West, May 10.—Spanish vessels are circling Cuba. Cuban towns are filling up, and rioting is prevalent

Supplies for Insurgents.

Special to the BULLETIN.

Tampa, Fla., May 10.—The steamer Gussie left here this morning for Cuba, with arms, ammunition and provisions for the insurgents. The United States is now supplying the insurgents with arms, which will greatly strengthen them.

Spanish Fleet Heard From.

Special to the BULLETIN.

Washington, May 10.—The Spanish fleet is reported as being at the Windward islands today, southeast of Porto Rico.

Rations for Troops.

Special to the BULLETIN.

San Francisco, May 10.—Captain Baldwin has been ordered by the war department to purchase one million rations for the use of the troops for the Philippines.

Vessels Chartered

Special to the BULLETIN.

Washington, May 10.—The war department has chartered thirty vessels to be used in transporting troops to Cuba   The entire army starts from Chickamauga.

Bread Riots in Spain.

Special to the BULLETIN.

Madrid, May 10.—More bread riots have occurred today in different parts of Spain. Prisons are crowded, and the inmates are breaking out. Many citizens have been killed, and houses burned. The militia is powerless.

On Cuban Soil.

Special to the BULLETIN.

Key West, May 10—Another successful landing has been made on Cuban soil by Americans, who have communicated with the insurgents

Oregon's Food for Starving Cubans.

Special to the BULLETIN.

Key West, May 10.—Two tons of provisions from Oregon's contribution were landed at Santa Clara, Cuba, and eagerly devoured by the hungry multitude.

Montego Reported Killed.

Special to the BULLETIN.

New York, May 10.—A Shanghai special says that Montego, the defeated Spanish admiral, has been killed by the populace, after escaping from Cavite.

Spanish Spy Drowned.

Special to the BULLETIN.

Key West, May 10.—A Spanish spy, captured by Americans, jumped overboard in the harbor here today, and was drowned.

Deliverance is Near.

Special to the BULLETIN.

Key West, May 10.—The insurgents in Cuba are joyfully celebrating the coming of American troops.

Targets for Uncle Sam.

Special to the BULLETIN.

Madrid, May 10.—The Spanish government has purchased two more warships.

Spanish Mines Destroyed.

Special to the BULLETIN.

Washington, May 10.—A cable today says that the Americans have destroyed several mines in Porto Rico harbor.

Riot at Manila.

Special to the BULLETIN

Washington, May 10.—A cable today says that Dewey is unable to control the insurgents, and that a riot is in progress at Manila.

Kenneth Root has put in a number of first class wheels for rent at Hood's Bicycle Den.

During the Spanish American War, the Courier produced a daily one page bulletin to keep the local citizenry advised of the progress of the war in Cuba. The last news media to be added were the two Grants Pass radio stations shown below.

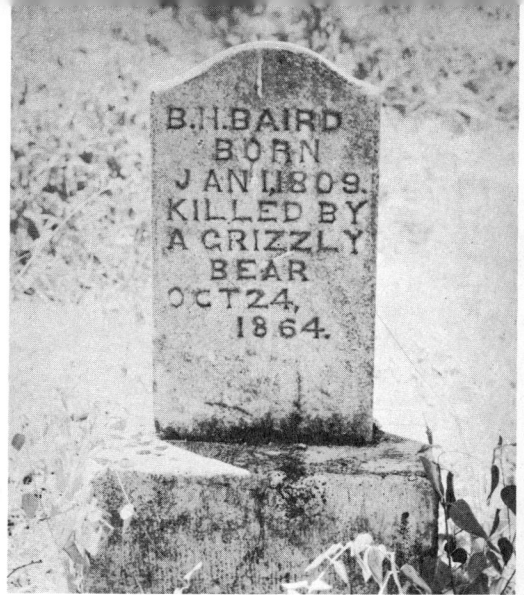

B. H. BAIRD
BORN
JAN 1,1809.
KILLED BY
A GRIZZLY
BEAR
OCT 24,
1864.

In the dedication picture on page one of this volume, Fred Isham is shown holding his grandfather's gun, bullet pouch and powder horn. These were the items carried by B. H. Baird (left above) when he was killed by a grizzly bear a short distance north of present Grants Pass. Baird was buried in the Croxton Cemetery (right above) and the old Pollock home (below) in which he died is shown below. This house is erroneously referred to in the 1910 Commercial Club brochure as General Grant's headquarters during the Indian Wars. For many years this caused confusing reports concerning the naming of the town, even though records available at that time proved conclusively that U. S. Grant had never been in the Rogue Valley during his west coast service at Forts Vancouver and Humbolt.

VII.
TRANSPORTATION

In Josephine's earliest years, all supplies were brought in by pack train. Some of the heavy articles were slung between two or more animals as shown above, while lumber for the mines was packed into the Althouse area as depicted below.

As the trails improved, freight wagons (above) brought dry goods and food stuffs into the county. A freight wagon and two trailers were known to have carried as much as 30 tons of goods. To warn others approaching a freight train on the same narrow one way trails, bells were mounted on the collars of lead animals (below). People living along the route of the freighters knew the identity of the driver long before he came into view because of the distinctively different bell tones used by each teamster.

Until 1914, the horse stage continued to serve as the primary method of transportation throughout Josephine County. When auto stages began service and were able to reduce the driving time between Crescent City and Grants Pass from 24 to 12 hours, the mud wagons began to disappear from service.

The Croxton Stage Station established in 1860 was located on Seventh Street a short distance north of Savage. The original stage barn is shown above. Ebenezzer Dimick, who ran the station for Croxton, is buried in the Croxton Cemetery (right). Many of the stage stations shown in this volume are far more elaborate than that of the mountain house (below) which served the stage line at the top of Mount Sexton.

EBENEZER DIMICK
1836 — 1900
SARAH J. HIS WIFE
1844 — 1915

The seemingly insurmountable task of completing the north-south railroad was resumed in 1882. Thousands of Chinese laborers (above) were employed in the work. To ease the steepness of the grades, many loop switchbacks like that at Wolf Creek (above) had to be designed.

Towering trestles (above) were built over the ravines, creeks and rivers.

The above scene shows a trestle under construction from both sides of the ravine. The trestles were anchored by fill dirt dumped after the construction had been completed (below).

The steep grades necessitated using two or more engines (above) whose wood burning fuel could be picked up along the right away and the hills adjoining the tracks became more bare as the years passed. New stations sprang up to allow service to remote mining areas of Josephine County. One of these, West Fork (below) provided the supplies needed at Galice and the lower Rogue Country.

The town of Grants Pass was selected for the building of the railroad repair shops. The picture above shows the engine turntable and a load of cord wood for locomotive fuel. The first through train from Portland arrived in Grants Pass on Christmas Eve of 1883, but due to the great difficulty encountered in completing the line over the Siskiyou Mountains, the first train from California (below) did not pass through Josephine County until 1887.

The first depot, the one across Sixth Street, that was moved to Merlin in 1896 or 1897. Picture taken on Royal Trestle.

After many years of complaints by the citizens of Grants Pass, the first station was removed from the center of Sixth Street and moved to Merlin where it is shown below.

MERLIN MEAT MARKET

MAIN ST. MERLIN, ORE.

MAP OF
JOSEPHINE COUNTY, OREGON.

The map above shows that portion of Josephine County served by the Oregon and California Railroad. This map appeared in an 1890 publication of Josephine County advertising its "livability".

Apparently there was an effort made to disguise the more picturesque name of Louse Creek by printing it as "Louise Creek".

The new railroad through Josephine County was plagued in its early years by many wrecks, such as the one shown above, which occurred near Wolf Creek. A Chicago, Illinois, land development company began early in the 1890's to exploit the Rogue Valley and potential buyers of speculation property were brought to Grants Pass on leased excursion trains (below).

Just prior to World Was I, a serious attempt was made to link Crescent City and Grants Pass by rail, which was the first effort in today's "Winnemucca-to-the-Sea" route. The California and Oregon Coast Railroad, for a short period of time, operated a few pieces of rolling stock (above) but found that passenger travel could just as easily be accommodated in the little gas powered "yellow peril" shown below.

C. & O.C.R.R.   Machine Shop   1914

Switch-back on the Redwood Highway between Grants Pass and Crescent. © 860

The terrain over which Oregon roads passed (above) for many years discouraged all but the more hardy from Crescent City to Grants Pass stage travel (right). Many who read this volume will hold vivid recollections of the old route over Mount Sexton shown below.

Pacific Highway on Sexton Mt. near Grants Pass.

The days of "car sickness" came to a close with the widening and straightening of the route over Mount Sexton (left above) and today's four lane highway (right above) makes the trip through Josephine a most pleasant one. The county's first steam roller is shown at the left and one of the beautiful county highways into the formerly inaccessible Galice region is shown below.

In 1923, the air age came to Grants Pass
with the first commercial airplane flights
taking off from the American Legion
Air Field (above) now occupied by the
Industrial Park. The first aerial exhibi-
tion, however, was a balloon ascension,
terminated by a parachute jump, in 1903
(right). The present Grants Pass Air-
port (below) serves visiting planes at
Harris Flat, northeast of Merlin.

VIII.
MINING

The mining of gold in the 1850's was responsible for the existence of Josephine County and has sporadically returned as a principal industry throughout the past century. In depression years, many families were able to remove their names from the welfare rolls by the use of the simple tools of the trade, namely, the shovel, pick and gold pan (plus much perspiration).

The hydraulic "giants" shown here were a familiar sight throughout Josephine County.

The Cameron-Simmons Mine near old Waldo was a prolific producer of gold ingots shown at the right. After the turn of the century, this became the Esterly property, whose offices are shown above. The mine was served by water tunneled through the mountain between Allen's Gulch and Waldo which flowed to the property through many miles of hand dug ditches. One of the county's earliest water turbine powered electric power plants (below) was installed here.

The richest mining area of Josephine County lay in the Althouse and Democrat Gulch regions of the Illinois Valley. Nothing remains of the original principal mining camp called Browntown, though a tourist attraction using the Browntown name (formerly the much later community of Tiger Town shown above) has remained as a tourist attraction and stands a short distance beyond the site of "Webfoot" Brown's General Merchandise Store. The old hotel and store at Holland (below), which stood at the foot of the Democrat Gulch trail, served the needs of the later miners after the demise of Browntown.

The earliest Althouse General Store is shown above. Hardrock mining reached its peak in the 1860's and miles of tunnels (below) were dug into the hills of Josephine County.

The first arrastras used to break up quartz rock were mule or water powered (above) but increasingly heavy production of ore brought steam powered stamp mills as shown below.

By the 1900's the mines had become an almost self-contained city (above) and new equipment was introduced in the underground mining operations (below). These are scenes of the famous "Greenback Mine".

The Granite Hill Mine operated one
of the largest stamp mill installations
in Josephine County (above).

Though gold production had become an industry dominated by big companies, small producers continued to operate throughout the valley, as we see in these scenes.

In many of the rubbish piles of Josephine County's extinct gold camps can be found artifacts left by Chinese miners who worked the areas after the white men deserted their claims to seek greater riches in Canada's Frazier River country or the mines of Idaho. Among the articles shown above are opium containers, pottery, opium pipes, and remains of once exquisite dishware. Gin Lin (right), best known for his later mining operations in the Applegate River region of Jackson County, first began mining in the Galice region where store records referred to him as Chiney Lin.

The last big producer of gold in the Galice area was the Alameda Mine shown on pages 110 and 111. Access to the mine was gained over the floating bridge across the Rogue shown above.

Throughout the valley can be seen the scars left by the floating dredges (above and page 112). These huge scows created their own small lakes as they moved from one point to another. One dredge, which overturned in its working area, for many years lay in front of the present home of the Alpine Meat Company at Grants Pass (below).

PORT SIDE

FRONT VIEW SHOWING BUCKET BELT

STERN VIEW SHOWING PUMP AND GOLD SAVING SLUICE BOXES

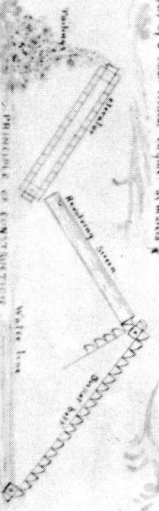

INTERIOR VIEW

PRINCIPLE OF CONSTRUCTION

HICKLER AND BARREY'S DREDGER
Now operating on
ROGUE RIVER

Placer Gold Mining Near Grants Pass Oregon.

The Dry Diggings Mine, which for many years after the mining had ended served as the Grants Pass Sanitary Dump northeast of town (above), received much of its water from the pipe line originating at Ament Dam (below).

The Ament Dam, built by the Golden Drift Mining Company served to provide both mining and irrigation water shortly after the turn of the century. News releases of the 1920's state that when a log jam developed, it was necessary to set dynamite charges and open the dam by blasting. Folklore advises that some investors wanted the dam removed to develop a need for the present one at Savage Rapids and contracted for the Ament Dam's removal.

The above scene shows the piping which carried water beyond present A Street for irrigation and mining operations. The scene below shows that section of the dam still standing. The planned electric powerhouse generators were never installed.

Because the costs of production have more than tripled since the price of gold was established some thirty odd years ago, little mining activity can be found in Josephine County today. In a few remote sections, however, a few of those ditches dug more than a hundred years ago to carry water to placer and hydraulic operations are still in use by modern day prospectors (above). Those adventurous enough to leave the main paved highways, may find an ingenious "self-shooter", like that shown below, still being operated in the same old mining method devised a century ago.

In depression years, amazing "Yankee ingenuity" was displayed in the revamping of discarded parts to build the arrastra shown at the left above. Some of Josephine's abandoned mines still have equipment lying dormant that somehow was overlooked in the war scrap drives (right above). Shortly after World War I, divers using the standard gear of hard hats and rubberized suits tried to mine many of the Josephine County rivers including the Rogue. Following World War II, the modern skin diving gear (below) has been used for this mining technique with much more comfort to the gold seeker. A short distance up Coyote Creek stood the town of Golden, a mining community of the 1890's (top of page 119). Though the picture of the hydraulic in full operation (also shown on page 119) could easily be mistaken for one of those at the early part of this chapter, this picture was taken within the last decade.

TAKILMA SMELTER

The Queen of Bronze Mine at Takilma dates its copper producing days back to the 1860's. All that remains of the smelter today is shown in the picture above. The scene at the right shows the same area when the smelter was in full operation. Until the building of the C & O C Railroad to Waters Creek, ore from the "Queen" was brought into the railhead at Grants Pass by freight wagons (below).

One mining process still in operation is the production of limestone from Marble Mountain to supply the needs of the cement plant at Gold Hill. The crushed rock is hauled down the mountainside in tram cars and dumped into the tipple (left above). The earliest limestone mining in Josephine County began in the Williams area, then called Williamsburg. Prior to this activity, gold had been mined in that area since 1859. When Oregon was invited to provide a marble block to be included in the construction of the Washington Monument (right above) the stone was selected from the quarry at Williams. The block, with its Oregon state seal (below) is mounted in the west wall at the 325 foot level above ground.

Josephine County is dotted with mulchy sawdust piles and brush choked clearings which mark the sites of remote lumbering operations. Huge stumps, cut above the butt swell by long departed fallers using springboards (page 122) still stand in Josephine's forests. The earliest sawmills in the county were the whip-saw variety as shown above and logs were hauled to the mill by teams of oxen as shown below.

SUGAR PINE MILL, JOSEPHINE CO.

Oxen were used for the heavy hauling on rough terrain or in the mill areas as shown above. The scene below shows oxen, horse, and mule teams all in use during the same era. The pictures on page 125 show water powered "woodpecker" or "mulay" whip sawmills through which the logs were pushed with a "peavey". The saw blade cut on the down stroke and could produce almost 1200 board feet of lumber on trouble-free days.

An early sawmill with circular blades is shown above. The lower picture shows a typical small sawmill such as existed in great numbers throughout Josephine County during the years of World War II. The two modern plants shown on p. 127 are Josephine Plywood, formerly Grants Pass Plywood (above) and the lumber and plywood producing Bates Lumber at Merlin (below).

Some of the early mills also diversified their production by manufacturing roof shingles (above) and window sash (below).

The steam donkey (above) was used to drag logs to a central loading area by cable winching them from the surrounding forest. Other ingenious methods devised to move logs to the mill included homemade railroads with rails assembled from logs as shown below.

Log wagons with steel banded tree cross sections for wheels (above) were used to supply the mills. The sawing was usually done adjacent to the harvesting areas and horse drawn wagons (below) hauled the lumber to shipping points.

Wood burning steam tractors (above)
replaced the horse and were in turn
replaced by the gasoline truck (below).

U.S. POST OFFICE, HOLLAND, ORE.
HARRY R. FLOYD
GENERAL MERCHANDISE

The trestle supported wooden flume shown above was located in the Jump-off-Joe region of Josephine County and its water lubricated trough carried rough lumber for a distance of 11 miles through the rough terrain (below) to the steam powered planing mill of Three Pines Timber Company.

Three Pines Mill was located on the Southern Pacific right-of-way between Merlin and Hugo (above). The walkways shown in the view at left below were constantly patrolled to prevent flumed lumber from jamming. A pile up could occur very quickly and the flume would overflow, washing out the foundations of the supporting trestle requiring expensive repairs. World War I brought the gasoline powered truck (right below) into the logging operations.

The ancient art of axmanship (above) and two man crosscut sawing ended with the introduction of the power saw (below).

When the modern faller has completed his job, the "bucker" measures and cuts the tree to specified lengths (above). The chore of hauling to the landing, once done by oxen or horses has been taken over by huge caterpillar tractors (right). At the loading stations the same crane that unloads the trailer brought "piggyback" on the truck's return to the woods (left below) is used to load the carrier (right below).

Though no longer a common sight, Josephine County residents occasionally see logs containing enough timber to build several homes (above) being hauled as a single load. Modern "stackers" (left) are used to load box cars when the latter are available (a "shortage" has existed since 1903). The thinning operations of the "perpetual harvest" plan provide Christmas trees for many of the major west coast cities (below).

To combat the greatest danger to Josephine's prime natural resource, fire lookouts have long been a part of the county's landscape (above). Hundreds of potentially disastrous fires have been averted by the alertness of these guardians of our forests with the aid of the newest branch of the Forest Service, the "smoke jumpers" (right and below) from Cave Junction.

X.
AGRICULTURE

The early settlers called the Rogue Valley "the Italy of Oregon". Few areas have proven to be so capable of successfully producing such a wide variety of farm crops (above). The first farming began in the Illinois Valley to provide vegetables needed by the miners, but before a decade had passed, hundreds of acres were being cleared for the new industry.

Tree stumps were removed from fields as shown above and crops of hay (left and below) were among the first commercial ventures.

The first grist mill in Josephine County began to grind flour in 1857 at Kerby (above). Hops were among the first Grants Pass crops (right).

Whole families gathered to work as crews in the picking season (above) and the pickers' pay was determined in the field (right). Josephine County farms, like the one shown below, produced 70,000 lbs. of hops in 1888.

The first carload of watermelons were shipped from Josephine County in 1892 (above and left). Not all of the melons found their way to market (below).

Other varieties of melons were grown in abundance (above). Until after the turn of the century few farms of Josephine County had mechanized their operations.

Steam power first made its appearance on the farms to power the threshers (above). The caterpiller tractor (right) was used for every job once performed by horses (left). The modern baler (below) makes haying look almost easy.

Josephine County was well on its way to being Oregon's major apple producer when the railroads raised their freight rates to a point that the growers destroyed their orchards and turned to other crops. Before the end of World War I the number of orchards had been reduced by 90 per cent of the pre-war number.

15,000 BOXES
JOSEPHINE CO.
APPLES
READY TO PACK FOR
CHINA

The scene above shows the preparation of apples for shipment to China. The canning of tomatoes (left) was done in the Grants Pass plant shown at the left of the picture below.

Unloading a car of Tokay grape roots and cuttings (127,000 vines) at Grants Pass for planting in this section.

In 1906 Tokay grapes became the popular agricultural venture. Tokay Heights and the Grants Pass High School yearbook (spelled Toka) still remain as reminders of Josephine's prolific vineyards. Irrigation has played an important role in the county's agricultural history. Many of the hand dug ditches (below) are still used today.

To provide a more adequate water system for the Grants Pass area, Savage Rapids (above) was chosen as the site for a new dam (below).

The Savage Rapids Dam (above) was completed two years after the loss of Ament Dam (at Pierce Riffle). The structure was raised in the 1950's to hold back a greater body of water (below).

These pictures could best be titled "Life on the farm in Josephine County".

Holland was the site of one of the county's earliest butter producing creameries (above). The county has long been noted for its high producing dairy herds (right) and Rogue Gold Cheese (below) has established a tradition for its excellence.

Beef cattle (above) are still driven to open ranges to graze and the branding of calves still remains a part of the Josephine cattle rancher's life (left). "Bummer lamb care" has not changed either (below).

The need for a "clearing house" of farming knowledge was met with the establishment of Josephine's first grange at Deer Creek (above left) in 1907. Among the ideas exchanged was the use of Marble Mountain limestone for fertilizer (above right), silage storage (left). Efforts in diversification of crops led eventually to development of the vast mint farm (below) near the junction of the Applegate and Rogue Rivers.

Gladiola bulbs (above) and cut flowers (left) have provided the most beautiful of the Rogue valley crops. The brilliant floats of yesteryear's "Glad Parade" (below) attracted visitors from hundreds of miles away.

Each year the agricultural accomplish-
ments of Josephine County are displayed
at the fairgrounds in Grants Pass (above
and below).

XI.
INDUSTRY

One of the earliest Grants Pass factories was the Pacific Pine Needle Company (above) whose products were used for pillows and similar items. The local "cigar factory" (left) was located at 5th and G streets.

The manufacture of brick (above) played an important role in the rebuilding programs sparked by the fires of 1894, 1899, 1902 and 1907. Home delivery of meat products (right) was provided cheerfully. During the hot summer months, the delivery wagon from the ice plant (below) drew crowds of youngsters like a magnet.

Before 1900, the commercial salmon fishing fleet (above) had been well established. The fishermen used gill nets until seigning was adopted in 1905.

The above scene shows the cleaning
of salmon while the picture below represents a single day's catch.

Commercial catches were salted and packed in barrels (above) for shipment to Portland and San Francisco. During this same period the United States government began one of its first ventures into the fish hatching field and established facilities on the Applegate River (below).

The boats shown above were used by the hatchery to catch steelhead and salmon. The fish were placed in holding pens (left below) until they were ready to spawn. With the meager knowledge of fish life then available, it was not known that the eggs could be expelled without killing the female and "killing days" were held throughout the spawning season (right below).

The public was invited to pick up the stripped fish at no charge (above) and the "killing days" were well attended. The eggs were fertilized (left below) and placed in holding troughs (right below) for hatching or shipment to other regions. Eggs were sent to points as far away as South America.

In 1915 a sugar refinery (above) began operation on the south side of the Rogue River near Grants Pass. One old industry, Trimble's Blacksmith Shop gave way to the modern present home of the U. S. National Bank in 1956.

Blacksmithing is one of Josephine's oldest industries (above) which still continues to flourish through the automobile age. The endless efforts to improve our highways has required the constant expansion of sand and gravel companies (right below).

With the vastly improved highways modern shopping centers (above) are easily reached and the travel urge can truly become an obsession while viewing the products of Caveman Camper (right) at the north end of Grants Pass' Industrial Park (below).

XII.
RECREATION

Undoubtedly the earliest form of "recreation" in towns which served the mines were such hospitality centers as the Kerby Buckhorn (left above). Tokens known as "brass checks" were issued for many goods and services (right above), frequently taking the place of money. The ladies of the community spent less exciting evenings at "quilting bees" (below).

Sunday was meeting day at the general store (Murphy shown above). No Washington Day celebration was complete without a ball (right). The 1914 rodeo at Holland was made a bit more difficult for mounting riders because of the lack of chutes (below).

Important dignitaries were patiently a-
waited by the crowds at the railroad
station (above), while those seeking the
serenity of a drive through the majestic
Redwoods to Crescent City (below)
could rent a rig at the "Red Barn"
(left) to make the trip.

The first fraternal order established at Kerby was the Belt Lodge No. 18 A.F. & A.M. The Masonic hall first used was the barn above until more spacious quarters (right) had been completed. The present lodge meetings are held in the 1902 building right of center in the Kerby street scene below.

In yesteryear, any occasion called for a parade. Kerby had its Indian Veterans Day (above) while Grants Pass had its Rose Festival (left). The Grants Pass affairs have become more formal through the years (page 171). Kerby's later parades were still a bit dusty (below).

In the lake behind the old 1892 power dam, boating meant a leisurely cruise upriver (above) while a dip in the Rogue River was more formal (left) but less well attended than today's Caveman Pool (below).

Fishing as well as boating was observed faithfully by fishermen with a bench provided for dull fishing days (above). A baseball bat could be used as a fishing pole and also carry the prize home (right), though some catches necessitated a longer carrying rod (below).

Those living beside the Rogue usually could be found sleeping near their salmon board (above), willing to be a-wakened if a fish of the size shown at left were in the vicinity. Unfortunately some "catches" (left below) looked much like today's and the real fishermen went "down river" (right below) to find the "big ones".

Modern fishermen employ "river guides" today and often pass Zane Grey's old cabin (above) in their quest of salmon and steelhead. The annual Memorial Day hydroplane race to Galice (left and below) usually restricts the trolling fisherman until the water subsides.

Deer are plentiful in Josephine County. The above shows the results of a day's hunt.

Viewing the "day's hunt" (left above) we are amazed that any deer still remain in Josephine County. In depression years the really proficient hunters could earn up to $10.00 by "helping" some less proficient marksman (right above). Exhibition precision riding by the Timber Riders and Josephine County Sheriffs Posse shown at the left can only be exceeded in excitment by the speeding sulkey or the "Sport of Kings".

Josephine County square dances are well attended (left above) but the younger set often prefer midget racers (right above) or the high speed motorcycles (right). Josephine residents still relish a good barbecue like this Josephine County Historical Society meeting of 1965 (below).

Barbecues and "potlucks" have long been popular in Josephine County and the affairs of yesteryear were always attended by "China" Bow, last of the county's Chinese miners (left and left below). The meat course (right below) was usually in ample supply.

The "home barbeque" is really not so new (above), and urge to travel on the newly graded and gravelled roads (right) could be gratified if you owned a little camping gear (below).

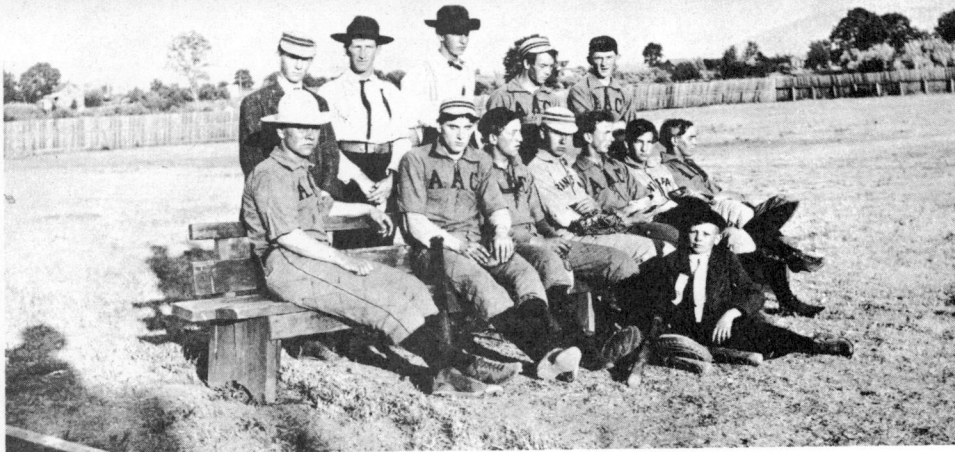

The uniformed baseball teams of Grants
Pass (above) and Murphy (left) en-
tertained the spectators at the Sixth
Street Grants Pass ballpark (south of
M Street). The Placer miners ball club
is shown below.

While horseback riding (above) was an all year form of recreation, winter sports (right) were not too far distant from any Josephine community. In 1926 a new 9 hole golf course near Grants Pass (below) was completed to round out the summer recreation offerings.

XIII.
"IT'S THE CLIMATE"

For many years, a sign bearing the slogan "It's the Climate" spanned Grants Pass' Sixth Street to further acquaint the world with one of the specific natural blessings enjoyed by Josephine County. An even earlier wooden arch (above) proudly proclaimed ours to be the "Finest Climate". Though the county's total record definitely attests to the validity of these claims, no history could be considered honest or complete if mention of nature's less kindly acts were not included.

The year of 1890 brought one of the heaviest snowstorms known until that date (above and below). It has been said that the depth on the valley floor exceeded four feet.

Snow Storm 1890 - Grants Pass, Ore.

Grant's Pass Bridge 6th St. taken Flood Feb. 1890.

Warm winds and rain brought a sudden runoff of more water than had been seen in all of Josephine County's previous history. The first Grants Pass bridge (above) completed just four years before, was swept away in the raging torrent, leaving only the southern approach standing (below).

Flood Rogue River - View from 6th St. Grant's Pass, Or.

This same 1890 flood brought destruction to Kerby (above). The year 1927 brought another heavy flood to Josephine County and the picture below was taken at Rough and Ready Creek during this storm.

A long standing argument regarding the usefulness of the Grants Pass railroad bridge across the Rogue River was settled permanently by the Christmas Day flood of 1955 (above). In the 1964 picture below it is a little difficult to realize that the normal water level lies more than thirty feet below the bottom supports of the Hellsgate bridge.

Man made and lightening ignited forest
fires have taken their toll throughout
the county. One of the most disasterous
was the Rough and Ready Creek burn
of 1918. One of the most recent was
the Wilderville fire of 1959 (above).
The Columbus Day gale of 1962 (right
and below) produced wind velocities
which had not been experienced in the
county since half of the marketable
timber in Josephine was blown down
in 1892.

Grants Pass with its excellent tourist facilities (above) has catered to the travelling public (left) since building its first "auto camp" in 1925. The earlier hotel accomodations (above, page 189) left something to be desired, but the 1923 Oregon Caves Resort (below page 189) provided a rustic setting in beautiful surroundings quite in advance of its time.

The present Chateau (above) is majestic in its setting of natural forest beauty. The thousands of yearly visitors (left) to Josephine's National Monument pass through the county's newest town, Cave Junction (left below) on their visit to the Caves. One of the most beautiful parks in the county is that in the city of Grants Pass (right below).

Few counties in the state, if any, have provided their citizens and the visitor with such pleasant and useable family recreational facilities as are to be found at Josephine's Lake Selmac (above).

A short distance from what was Umpqua Joe's ferry (below) the Parks Department established another outstanding camping and picnicking area on the Rogue River.

Historic
INDIAN MARY PARK

Smallest Indian Reservation ever created,
granted to Indian Mary by U.S. Government
in 1885 in recognition of gratitude to her father,
Umpqua Joe, who gave the alarm which saved
white settlers of this area from a planned massacre.

•

CAMPING PICNICKING SWIMMING
Rest Room Facilities

Developed by the
JOSEPHINE COUNTY COURT and
the **JOSEPHINE COUNTY PARK BOARD**

•

The park sign (left above) briefly
sketches the story of Indian Mary,
shown with her daughter at the right
above. An aerial view of the park is
presented below.

Credit for initially making the Galice area accessible to tourists must be given the C.C.C. groups at Camp Rand (above) who completed a swinging bridge (left) across the Rogue at Grave Creek in 1935. The bridge served the motoring public until it was replaced in 1965 with a modern concrete structure (below).

Other Josephine County Civilian Conservation Corps camps were located at Williams and Camp Greyback. All that remains of the latter's efforts is a single building and a lone chimney (left above) to mark the camp's site. One visitor's facility at Greyback Forest Camp, built by the Corps, still serves today (above). Some work begun by the original Corps has been picked up by today's Job Corps at Fort Vannoy (left and below).

A visitor's "must see" is the admission free Josephine County Historical Museum in Kerby (above). Dorothy Darneille (right) in cooperation with the Josephine County Library prepared the permanent displays of Indian artifacts for library use. Donley Barnes, Society president (left below) is shown with the rare "Oregon Boot", a device once used to discourage "tourism" ideas among the early Josephine County jail "guests". The president, the Society and the author (right below) join with the Publications Chairman in extending thanks to all who made this historical unit a reality.

XV.
FIRST CENTURY OF RECORDED ROGUE VALLEY HISTORY

The first century of recorded Rogue valley history, 1825 to 1925:

1825 Hudson's Bay trappers under Thomas McKay and Finan McDonald followed Indian trails through Rogue valley to McCloud and Scott Rivers of California.

1828 A Hudson's Bay fur brigade, under Alexander Roderick McLeod, from Fort Vancouver, crossed the Rogue River near Grants Pass (Fort Vannoy) on return from California.

The Oregon Historical Society attributes the naming of Jump-Off-Joe Creek to an accident involving a member of this brigade, Joe McLoughlin, a step-son of the Chief Factor at Vancouver, Dr. John McLoughlin.

1835 George Gay, a survivor of the Jedediah Smith party massacre, with a Hudson's Bay trapping party enroute to their outpost near Yreka, was attacked near Foots Creek.

1836 Ewing Young and party bring cattle north from California through Rogue River valley. Attack by Indians near Foots Creek resulted in loss of one cow.

1841 Lt. Emmons, an officer of the Exploring Squadron of Charles Wilkes, led an expedition through the Rogue valley enroute to Yerba Buena (San Francisco).

1844 California settlers, led by Stephen Meek, followed Hudson's Bay trail north to Willamette valley.

1846 Jesse and Lindsay Applegate and Levi Scott and party passed through Rogue valley when establishing a southern route to Fort Hall, Idaho.

Martha Leland Crowley of the first emigrant train to try the Applegate Trail, died and was buried on the north bank of a stream named Grave Creek.

1848 Peter Burnett with 150 men ("Burnett's Ragged Regiment") passed through valley enroute to California gold fields.

Another Sacramento bound party under James Nesmith discovered the remains of Martha Crowley, disinterred by Indians for her clothing. They reburied the bones beside an oak tree on the north bank of Grave Creek.

1850 General Joseph Lane, first territorial governor of Oregon, came to Rogue valley and made peace treaty with Rogue River Indians (June).

In spring of 1850 more than 200 miners were seeking gold in Rogue and Umpqua valleys.

Following the signing of the Indian treaty, whites began to settle in the valley and a man by the name of Long built a ferry a few miles west of present Grants Pass (Fort Vannoy).

1851 Josephine Rollins, after whom the county is named, her father, Floyd Rollins, and other prospectors, come to the Illinois valley. Their party (from the state of Illinois) is credited with having made the first discovery of gold in southern Oregon (on Josephine Creek). The party was taken to the site by Indians they met near Vannoy Crossing.

Port Orford on the coast was selected as the logical location from which soldiers could protect Rogue River settlers and Ford Orford was built.

Indian raids result in military reprisals at Stuart Creek (Bear Creek) and the first battle at Table Rock.

Governor Gaines came to the valley to make second treaty with the Rogue Rivers.

1852 Jackson County, including all of what was later to be Josephine County, was formed by the territorial legislature.

Gold discovered at Sailor Diggings (Waldo) when sailors who "jumped" ship at Crescent City came inland toward Jacksonville, resulting in the district's biggest gold rush.

Gold discovered on Althouse Creek.

Gold discovered on Galice Creek, reputedly by Dr. Louis Galice.

First ditch for hydraulic mining in Illinois valley was built at Allen's Gulch (Waldo).

Sam, chief of the Table Rock band, declared war on settlers because he claimed a white man settled on land Indians used for winter camp and because a white man refused to betroth his two year old daughter to Sam's son.

Indian battle at Big Bar.

1853 This was the year of "Starvation Winter" when heavy snow closed all trails into the valley and a "pinch" of salt was traded even for a "pinch" of gold.

Gold discovered in Democrat Gulch and Browntown was established by "Webfoot" Brown who operated a general merchandise store.

Indian War of 1853 caused the settlers to erect stockades around forts Briggs and Elizabeth (renamed Fort Hayes) and last known as Anderson Stage Station near Selma.

Matthew P. Deady appointed first associate territorial justice for southern Oregon district, including what is later Josephine County, held court at the "village of Waldo".

Indian battles at Table Rock, Williams, and Evans Creek.

First pack train trail opened between Illinois valley and Crescent City.

Peace treaty with Takelma tribes in council at Table Rock, establishing the Table Rock Reservation.

James Kerby took donation claim in Illinois valley on land where Kerby is later built.

James Vannoy bought Long's ferry.

Chief Taylor of the Grave Creek tribe hanged at Vannoy's ferry.

James Savage settled with bride on what was later to be named Savage Creek.

Nearest post office for Illinois valley was at Dardanelles (near Gold Hill).

1854 Orson Gilbert settled on a donation claim which included most of the land on which Grants Pass was later built.

First survey for a wagon road to the coast from the Illinois valley was made.

William Mooney filed the first donation claim on Deer Creek.

Trefethen and Holland began raising vegetables (first agricultural venture in valley) for miners at Browntown. Chinese miners had their own gardens before this venture began.

The California-Oregon boundary was finally defined in November. Until this time, the miners had voted in both California and Oregon elections but had not been paying taxes to either state.

An amendment to the Table Rock Treaty, made by the U. S. Congress, required all tribes of the Rogue valley to be placed on reserve regardless of language or traditional differences. All were to be thereafter known as the "Rogue River Indians".

Name of the Rogue River changed to "Gold River" by Oregon Territorial Legislature.

1855 Company of white men from Jacksonville, attack Indian camp on Butte Creek, killing most of the band which was comprised of old men, women, and children (October 8).
Indians go on warpath, killing at least 23 white persons the first day.

First major battle of the war was fought at Skull Bar, near the mouth of Galice Creek on Rogue River. Town of Galice Creek destroyed. Whites saved only by warning of Umpqua Joe.

Indians won indecisive battle at Hungry Hill near Grave Creek crossing.

Lotta Crabtree performed for Browntown miners. Used her dancing slippers to carry gold off the stage.

1856 Josephine County separated from Jackson by legislative act (January 22). First meeting of Board of County Commissioners.

James Hendershott chosen to be first sheriff of Josephine County.

First Kerby school house built.
Table Rock band and Umpqua Indians taken to Grande Ronde Reservation (near Yamhill River). Neither had engaged in the 1855 war.

Fort Lamerick erected near later Camp Rand CCC area.

Indian War ended in final battle near Agness. Tribes were moved to Siletz Reservation.

County seal adopted (September 1).

First Josephine County jury list drawn. Eighty seven men were listed, of which 37 were farmers, 39 miners, 1 packer, 3 blacksmiths and 2 butchers.

First Josephine County tax levy made, totaling 11 mills.
Waldo post office established.

First water right in county granted for Sucker Creek waters.

County commissioners grant first order for a legal publication to the "Herald" of Crescent City, there being no newspaper in Josephine County.

1857 County seat moved from Waldo to Kerbyville.

Construction on first wagon road to Crescent City from Illinois valley begun.

County court studies first road petition in Josephine County. Proposed road would run from Applegate Creek to Waldo via Mooney mountain.

Ballots at election show Josephine County vote as follows: Accepting state constitution, 445 for and 139 against; slavery 155 for and 435 against (November 7).

There were two churches in Illinois valley, a Catholic church at Allen's gulch and a Methodist church on Althouse Creek.

Methodist group organizes near where Grants Pass later established.

D. S. Holton first (recorded) county judge of probate. Dr. Holton had also been appointed the first coroner for the county. In this year he purchased the remaining half of James Kerby's land claim.

1858 Fort Vannoy school established. "Kerbyville still improving - liveliest town for one of its size in Oregon - two large stores, two splendid hotels, a livery stable, barber shop, and billiard saloon. All in successful operation. Stage from Crescent City every other day, generally loaded with passengers - often the returning bridegroom with bride."

Slate Creek (Wilderville) post office established.

Waldo had estimated population of 1500.

Western Star Lodge No. 18, A. F. and A. M. was organized at Kerbyville.

Col. Joseph Hooker, U. S. Army ("Fighting Joe" of the Civil War), built road through valley from Scottsburg to Camp Stuart (Central Point).

Irons for prisoners made by blacksmith Wm. Booth at cost of $24.00.

1859 Oregon admitted to the Union (February 14).

M. C. Barkwell became first county judge under the state government (June).

Williamsburg (later Williams) was founded as a mining town when "all gold bearing deposits in Josephine County had been worked and exhausted".

Kerbyville name was changed to "Napoleon" by the state legislature.

Belt Lodge No. 26 A. F. and A. M. was organized at Waldo.

Bridge built across Illinois at ranch of John W. Patrick. Tolls charged were:

Wagon and span of horses	25c
Additional span of horses	25c
Loaded horses and mules	25c
Man and horse	25c
All loose animals	10c
Sheep and hogs	5c

1860 Stage station moved to site of future Grants Pass as a team changing stop for the California Stage Company. (Had been at Jump-Off-Joe).

First Josephine County budget was adopted, placing expenses at $14,000.00 Revenue collected was $11,000.00 from taxable property, $1,000.00 from liquor and billiard licenses, $2,000.00 from Chinese licenses.

Wagon road from Waldo to Crescent City opened.

The presidential election was hotly contested in Southern Oregon due to the heavy concentration of slave holder sympathizers. Damage ranged from bloody noses and blackened eyes to torn suspenders in the lively polling place brawls. At Williams, it was necessary for the three men casting Lincoln votes to vote together while carrying guns.

1861 Post offices at Kerbyville, Leland, Slate Creek, Vannoy's, and Waldo.

1862 First big flood known to Josephine County history. (First recorded flood was 1853).

1863 "Greenbacks" worth less than 40 cents on the dollar. Josephine County tries to use same to pay state tax. State refused. Josephine County then refused to pay state tax.

1864 First Grants Pass school (near 10th and Savage) starts with 15 pupils. Methodist minister serving as teacher.

Queen of Bronze mine opened (Takilma).

Stage station and barn built at Grave Creek.

Chinese population of county was 700

Land on which Grants Pass was later built was originally filed upon by Orson Gilbert, purchased by Thomas Croxton.

1865 Post office established at ("Grant's Pass) after name of "Grant" had been refused by Post Office Department in Washington (feared possible confusion with Grant County, Oregon, approved during same year) Thomas Coxton first Postmaster.

Census of Josephine County shows the following figures: Total population 785. There were 329 legal voters in the county; 342 were males over 21 years old; 44 males under 21 years and over 10 years; 118 males under 10 years; there were 127 females over 18; 35 females under 18 and over 10; and 119 females under 10.

This year there were 16,033 ounces of gold dust produced in Josephine County.

1866 First bridge built across Jones Creek.

1867 Actual ground survey of Oregon-California boundary completed.

Burns school on south bank of Applegate River near Slate Creek erected for Wilderville district.

1868 Grants Pass voting precinct established by Jackson County Court at home of Thomas Croxton. Until this time, area was called the Perkinsville election precinct.

Grants Pass school district formed as Jackson County District #23.

1869 Kerbyville (Kerby) "center of Josephine County trade."

1870 Poll tax of $4.00 required to vote ($1.00 to state of Oregon, $1.00 for county fund and $2.00 for county welfare (paupers') hospital).

1871 "Public road" established between Rock Point Bridge to Josephine County line "about three miles below the old Hunter's ferry".

1872 Jackson County Court defined boundaries of Grants Pass election precinct as the boundaries included in all Township 35 and 36, S. Range 5, West and East to Evans Creek. Voting was to be done at house of E. Dimrick.

Since no newspapers were yet printed in Josephine County, the Democratic Times in Jacksonville was designated official publication for notices and advertisements.

1873 County road built between Kerby and Waldo.

County welfare allowance: "for keeping a county pauper 62 days . . . . the sum of $62.00".

1874 Oregon Caves discovered by Elijah Davidson (some accounts say in 1873).

1875 Population of Josephine county, according to the assessor, 1,132.

1876 Post office was established at Murphy.

Kendal and Bolt Store in Kerby rented to serve as County Courthouse (first Courthouse was log cabin of James Hendershott in Waldo, 1856).

Waterpowered sawmill built on Jackson Creek near Wilderville by Wetherbee.

Fruitdale school opened. Named Centennial School in honor of 100th year following the Declaration of Independence.

1877 "Town of Althouse was established.

Prices paid for deer hides at Kerby store was 15c per lb., otter skins $2.00 each. Freight cost this year was 2c per lb. Whiskey sold for $10.00 per case, eggs 20c per dozen, and wheat, 90c per bushel.

Price paid by County Court for pauper funerals was $10.00 for coffin and $10.50 for grave digging and burial.

1878 Slate Creek post office name changed to Wilderville.

1879 Wheat grown on land where Grants Pass now is.

Tax receipts for Josephine County, $8,330.27.
1880 Population of Josephine County, 2,400.

Boundary line between Josephine and Curry Counties defined.

1881 County indebtedness was $3,825.53. Outstanding warrants for this figure drew 10% interest. Debt included $1,421.09 for schools, $977.80 for roads and bridges and $870.60 to care for poor (welfare).

1882 Contract for construc ing the first county bridge across east fork of the Illinois let at $1,400.00.

Josephine County election precincts were Jump-Off-Joe, Slate Creek, Williamsburg, Kerbyville, and Althouse.

1883 Oregon and California (later Southern Pacific) railroad is completed to Grants Pass.

Grants Pass old original townsite surveyed by C. J. Howard. Effort made to rename town "Sugar Pine City".

First building in Grants Pass business section built at the corner of Sixth and G Streets.

First passenger train from Portland arrived on Christmas Eve.

Liquor license issued to Jesse Griffith "to sell spiritous liquors in the Grants Pass Precinct in quantities less than one quart". Fourteen licenses for retailing drinks by the glass were issued between 1880 and 1885.

1884 Two story building from Jerome Prairie moved to present Washington School site in Grants Pass to become Central School.

Voting place for present Grants Pass changed from "house of E. Dimmick to the new school house."

1885 Gin Linn & Company purchased English Company's mines at Galice. Gin Linn is listed as "Chiny Lin" in store records of 1856 at Galice and Althouse areas.

The "Argus", first newspaper of Josephine County printed for a few weeks and succeeded by forerunner of present Grants Pass Courier. New publications refer to Rogue Valley as "the Italy of Oregon".

Grants Pass incorporated.

Legislature changed the boundary line between Josephine and Jackson Counties, placing Grants Pass within Josephine County.

Grants Pass was made county seat of Josephine County.

1886 The Methodist Episcopal Church, first in Grants Pass, was completed.

First County Courthouse built in Grants Pass, completed at a cost of "$2,400.00 payable in gold coin or its equivalent in county warrants."

First county bridge built across Rogue River at Grants Pass is constructed at a cost of $7,000.00.

First county bridge to be built across the Applegate, near the mouth of Slate Creek, cost $3310.00.

J. H. Robinson establishes first high school building in Josephine County on his lower Applegate farm.

McAlliser post office (Merlin) established.

"From the Courier of August 6th we find that there are 135 residences and buildings used for residences; there are 51 business houses all told. Besides these, are the M. E. church, courthouse and jail, depot and warehouse, two livery stables, three windmills, town hall and rink, I. O. O. F., Masonic and I. O. G. T. lodge rooms, brewery (unfinished) sawmill, sash and door factory (size 50x125 feet), two stores, two bakeries, academy, two laundries, six-till round house, railroad machine shops, wagon shop, brick kiln, and a $10,000 bridge almost completed. Add to this 23 barns and we have 226 buildings in our little city and the town no more than 23 months old. This does not include a host of small buildings, nor do we count the railroad turn table and water tank."

1887 Skating rink built at Waldo.
Coroner, Dr. F. W. Van Dyke presented bill of $25.00 for postmortem examination of bodies of Umpqua Joe (written as "Joe Umpqua") and Albert Pico who shot and killed each other at Indian Mary's cabin.

Stock company formed to build Grants Pass Opera House.

Grants Pass City Band made debut.

Many Chinese leave Kerby, Waldo, and Althouse to work on California-Oregon railroad or Gasquet wagon road.

Horace Gasquet opened toll road to Illinois valley.

1888 70,000 lbs. of hops (at 10c per lb.) shipped from Josephine County.

1889 Grants Pass Water, Light, and Power Company began construction of a powerhouse on north bank of Rogue River (downstream from Caveman Bridge).

1890 Third major flood of county's history.

1891 Town of McAllister, School District #5, became Merlin.

1892 First street lights installed in Grants Pass.

Most severe wind storm experienced to that time in Southern Oregon, blew down half of the marketable timber in the county.

First carload of water melons shipped from county.

1893 $100,000.00 in gold bullion shipped annually from Grants Pass.

Original Grants Pass Railroad depot moved to Merlin.

First four Chinese pheasants purchased for $32.00 and released in Josephine County. Fine of $50.00 established for anyone shooting these birds.

Effort made to change name of Grants Pass to "Stanford".

1894 Grants Pass Academy renamed Grants Pass High School.

Twenty-five year patent, signed by Grover Cleveland, established smallest Indian reservation in United States for Indian Mary.

Grants Pass fire destroys most of business area on Front Street (G Street).

1895 Rogue River Telephone Company extended service to Grants Pass.

The warm sultry summer emphasized the dire need in Grants Pass for a city wide sewage system.

1896 Due to ocean shipment competition, lumber shipping costs to San Francisco reduced from $1.05 to .86 per 100 lbs.

1897 Pine Needle Factory opened in Grants Pass.

In the first legal hanging of Josephine County, L. W. Melson confessed to murder of Charles Perry while on the scaffold.

"Salmon are so thick in the rivers at present that some are spearing them from the bridges."

1898 Murphy irrigation ditch completed.

Round trip fare to Crescent City was $15.00 (stage coach).

1900 School District #7 appeared for first time in records. Tax for district was 11 mills.

New Laundry opened in Grants Pass in the "old music hall" (now the Grants Pass Laundry or American Linen).

1901 Telephone line from Grants Pass to Williams completed.

Grants Pass city council passed ordinance requiring city prisoners to work on streets and street commissioner empowered to use shakles or ball and chain when necessary.

1902 Indian War veterans of Oregon (1847-1856) entitled to pension of $8.00 per month.

Unsuccessful attempt made to "river drive" logs from Grants Pass to Gold Beach.

Pay scale for first year Grants Pass teachers set at $35.00 per month; assistant principal $40.00. After first year a pay raise to be given amounting to $5.00 per month. Similar raise of like amount at end of five and ten years of "continuous faithful service."

Sawmill built at site to construct Golden Drift Mine Company's dam.
$1,070,000.00 in gold production that year.

"Glendale is 'on the boom', at least 20 new structures and a $2,000.00 school house built this summer. Lumber to the new box factory is being flumed into town."

1903 Sugar Pine Door & Lumber Company unable to ship 40 carloads of lumber due to railroad car shortage.

Flood nearly as large as the 1890 disaster.

Southern Oregon Baseball League formed. Members of league included Ashland, Medford, Jacksonville and Grants Pass.

Two bands and huge crowd awaited arrival of train in Grants Pass to see Teddy Roosevelt. Engineer forgot to stop.

Carpenters and joiners established a shorter 9 hour day with hourly rate of 33-1/3 cents or $3.00 per day.

1904 Briggs gold strike, about 10 miles from Hollard in the Sucker Creek district. "Goldenview City" staked out beside claim.

1905 First commercial seining for Rogue River salmon. Gill nets used before this year.

Grants Pass had one saloon for each 500 segment of its population. Ordinance passed to restrict amount of saloons to that ratio.

1906 Wild hogs numerous in the Applegate and Williams areas.

Beginning of tokay grape history.

1907 New Grants Pass High School paper named TOKA in honor of grape industry. First Rose Carnival Parade in Grants Pass. First motion picture show opened on G Street.

Three Pines Lumber began operations on Jump-Off-Joe Creek. Flume built to chute lumber to mill for distance of four miles (extended to 11 mile length by 1909).

Commercial Club organized in Grants Pass.

1908 Telephone lines extended to Fruitdale.

1909 President Taft issued proclamation establishing Oregon Caves as a national monument.

1910 First Josephine County Fair held at Williams with exhibits from Kerby and Fruitdale.

1911 Forest nursery established near Waldo. 43,000 seedling trees including seven different varieties were shipped from the new tree farm the following year.

Ament Dam contsructed to provide irrigation and mining water at Dry Diggings (old Grants Pass sanitary dump).

First spike driven for Oregon & Oregon Coast Railroad.

1912 First county poultry show held in Grants Pass.

The Pacific Interior Company organized to build line to Crescent City by way of Williams.

Steel bridge built across Applegate at Murphy.

Southern Oregon Supply Company advertised men's suits for sale at $6.25.

Speed limit in Grants Pass set at 15 miles per hour. Fine for first violation was $50.00 or 25 days; second offense, $100.00 or 50 days; third, $150.00 or 75 days.

1913 $12,000.00 given by Carnegie Foundation to build county library.

Galice Road bridge built across Rogue (near present Indian Mary Park).

21,000 Christmas trees shipped from Hugo to Los Angeles market.

The salmon fishing fleet numbered 25 boats. Catches were shipped to Sacramento and Portland.

Klocker Printery opened for business.

1914 Library opens with 150 volumes.

"Modern Auto Stage" began service in competition to Crescent City stage coach. Bus driving time was 12 hours compared to horse stage's 24.

1915 Merlin fire destroyed all buildings in one full block.

C. & O.C. Railroad began passenger service between Wilderville and Grants Pass.

1916 Utah Beet Sugar Company built refinery in Grants Pass.

1917 $100,000.00 new Josephine County Courthouse completed in Grants Pass.

About 1300 tons of copper ore shipped from Queen of Bronze mine at Takilma.

"Selma is booming." Chrome mines down the Illinois were rapidly being opened up, pack trains were busy and a tent city of 50 tents was being built at the camp established to build the road.

1918 County authorized expenditure of $1200.00 per year for Public Library operation ($800.00 for books and remaining $400.00 for heat ,lights and janitor service.

From the Commissioners' Journal: "It is ordered that from this date, no dancing, vaudville shows or things of like character, be permitted in said (the county) Courthouse".

1919 Zane Grey fishing on Rogue River that season.

1920 A new electrified sign with the slogan "It's the climate" erected at 6th and G Streets in Grants Pass.

1921 Savage Rapids Dam began to provide irrigation water for the first time.

1922 Sexton Mountain highway "improved" to a 13 foot paved roadbed, edged with concrete curbs.

The Courier installed a radiophone receiving set. Ten stations could be picked up during the evening hours.

Pure gold bringing $20.67 per ounce.

Hop industry nets gross of $100,000.00. Thirteen carloads shipped to European ports.

Oregon Cavemen organized as Josephine County "booster" group.

1923 First commercial airplane flights from American Legion air field in Grants Pass.

Largest fish from the Rogue was a 47 lb. Chinook salmon.
Oregon Caves Resort incorporated and Caves Highway opened.

1924 Commercial Club became the Grants Pass Chamber of Commerce.

1925 One hundred dozen gladioli cut flowers shipped daily from Jewell ranch during blooming season.

Wolf Creek Tavern enlarged by addition of a wing to add 8 rooms and baths, making the resort a 20 room Tavern.

Large shipments of tomatoes and string beans. "Caveman" brand used on shipping crates and boxes.

Grants Pass Auto Camp accomodated 5,200 autos of tourists during the summer months.

OFFICERS

SYSTEMS SOFTWARE

An Introduction to Language Processors and Operating Systems

ELLIS HORWOOD SERIES IN COMPUTERS AND THEIR APPLICATIONS

Series Editor: IAN CHIVERS, Senior Analyst, The Computer Centre, King's College, London, and formerly Senior Programmer and Analyst, Imperial College of Science and Technology, University of London